How We Bury Our Dead

HOW WE BURY OUR DEAD

Faith Garbin

Negative Capability PRESS
MOBILE ALABAMA

How We Bury Our Dead

Founding Editor and Publisher
Dr. Sue Brannan Walker

Cover photograph by Katie Kelleher

Cover and Interior Design by Bailey Robertson
Edited by Bailey Robertson

ISBN 978-0-942544-35-0
Library of Congress Control Number: 2016902798

Negative Capability Press
62 Ridgelawn Drive East
Mobile, Alabama 36608
(251) 591-2922

www.negativecapabilitypress.org
facebook.com/negativecapabilitypress

For my daughters—
Megan and Katie—
who, as backwards as this may seem,
gave me life.

Table of Contents

Communion with the Dead

The House Laments the Loss of a Child

Uncle

God's Daughter Ushers in the End of the World

Plight

Casting the Bones

Communion with the Dead

FEBRUARY

is the month of bitter coldness,
of Valentines and dead presidents.
Groundhogs sniff the air; Dickens was born.

Father wheezes from the hospital bed.
Mother smokes outside, one cigarette,
then another. Windows shiver; ice clings.
Cardinals gather at the feeder,
peck at the empty bowl
the way Father gasps for air.

I imagine him dreaming—
of oxygen,
of words not spoken.

Mother pushes into the room,
ashes on her coat cuff.
Stomps her boots on the linoleum
floor as if to shake off
February's grasp; as if to awaken
the bed's shadow.

WHEN MY HUSBAND DIED

When my husband died, things somehow fell apart.
Sunlight slipped past the venetian blinds
and exposed patches of mold.
Termites swarmed in the dryer vent,
and abandoned their gossamer wings.
At night, I hear them feast on the house's bones.
The leaves have fallen to the ground
like a thousand bodies.
Yesterday, the coffee carafe
exploded like a heart.

Now I sleep alone trying
to unshare a double bed.
The stale sheets entangle me
in their private lives.
My dreams hide under the floorboards;
when I call out to them,
they fold themselves under pillows
where nightmares are born.
Before my husband died, the house
was a womb with two hearts beating.

AT THAT MOMENT

And what were you thinking
    at that moment
when your soul popped
    out of your body
breaking through
    invisible threads
that bound you here
    this space, this time
leaving behind the cumbersome
    heaviness of being.

And the pain, agonizing pain
    the price you paid
for your soul's release.

I was driving home from work
    at that moment
over a high rise bridge
    awed by a resplendent sunset
unknowingly celebrating
    your spiritual rebirth
a crescent moon
    hanging in the balance
overcome by joy
    the sheer joy of being.

DEATHBED

I roll your bed by the window,
blinds raised like eyelids.
You cough up the night like blood.

The moon inches its way toward morning,
powdering your face with light.
I nap in the rocking chair, and awaken

to find you sleeping, your veiny hands clenched,
pulling the sheets—your mouth, a parched
desert. Where are you now, Father?

Where have your dreams taken you?
Back to your father's house, memories
pried loose like the floorboards? Why

stumble over that ancient betrayal—
that same old pummeling of fists,
a whiskey bottle tipping the balance?

I remember your stories, how hope
spilled on the hardwood floor, slipped
between the cracks like water.

Sleep, Father, the dreamless sleep
of the guiltless. Let the night
pin the moon to the sky,

let the night break out in a hive
of stars. I will close the blinds.
There is nothing more to learn.

TO MY DEAD FATHER ON HIS BIRTHDAY

If you can visit, wear your Old Spice cologne.
I'll fold the towels into squares with razor-
sharp edges, the way you liked them in the
Army. After your shower, you can change
into comfortable clothing, cotton—not brown
like the dirt you've been hibernating under—
but blue like the sky, like infinite possibilities.
We can walk to Stan's on 42nd street where
Mother pawned your Gibson. We'll walk back
to my place, hand in hand, and I will bake you
a pineapple upside down cake, and the dough
won't be soggy. I'll use one candle, just for today.
You can play the guitar as I sing "Happy Birthday"
off-key, and if you tease me, I promise not to cry.
If you visit, the shutters on my windows will stop
grieving. Sunlight will pour in. We can sit cross-
legged on the floor and look at photo albums—
those sepia pictures of grown-ups who don't smile.
I'll even ask you: *Who is this person?* I will listen
to our family histories. You can tell all your stories
about the one-room schoolhouse and the day when
your brother woke up with polio. If you get bored,
we can play badminton out front on the lawn until
our feet are soaked with dew. I have a screened-
in porch where I'll serve coffee—decaf, black—
the way you like it. We can stare at the ravaged
moon. You can tell me, again, you don't believe
we ever walked on it, and I won't argue with you.
Later, you can lie on the couch in your Superman
boxer shorts, and I'll turn the air down until icicles
form on the ceiling. If you want to, you can fall
asleep to the drone of Fox News, the blue light
flickering like a K-Mart special. But before you
sleep, I need to know: what was the punch line
to the joke you started to tell in the hospital—
the one with the skinny man and the cannibal?

THAT FIRST NIGHT

The fan pushes stale air
from one side of the bedroom
to the other. Do the dead
hum as monotonously?
I listen for words, for a message,
but this is not a language I understand.
Tomorrow, I will remove my wedding ring.
I don't think the dead are sensitive,
or how could they leave us?

DOGWOODS

The winter you learned to let go of your body
was the winter I learned how to keep everything inside,
how to press satin pillows against my mouth
in the middle of the night, how to apply lipstick
in two strokes and drive to the theater—
a resentful daughter in the back seat—
batter our imaginations with happy endings
and forever afters. How to pack each piece of you
in a Goodwill box and silently watch
that thirteen-year-old hate me
just because I survived.

The winter you freed yourself of this life
was the winter I learned
about gentleness and homemade offerings.
It was time to let small gestures
fill a cavernous heart.

Upstairs, the neighbor's puppy was barking,
the woman in 12B brought chili in a chipped
bowl. In the courtyard, dogwood trees bloomed
with cardinals. At night, the old man below
strummed his guitar. I opened the patio door
and wondered: how could he play like that
in the dead of winter? How did his heart
rise above the cold?

COMPANION

She's here tonight, my mother, pacing behind
the bedroom door. Her footsteps are muffled
against the carpet, a sliver of light the only
illumination between us. Outside, the clouds,
a pewter gray, smother the sun; their shadows
are the coffins I feared as a child, when, after
a flood, the earth spit them out, stacked them
like dominoes against the mausoleum wall.
The neighbors wailed for days. Their keening
even alarmed the stoic crows.

Often mother paces alone in this house
where she married father. Depression
is her closest companion now, though
certainly there are pictures she can thumb
through, multi-colored albums neatly lining
the bookcase, touching the rigid wall.
Her memories form an album of their own,
in Kodachrome, like the maple trees in autumn—
leaves blazing as though preparing to
be shaken from the limbs that hold them.

INTERPRETER OF DREAMS

Grandmother moans
in her sleep
utters words
that are foreign
to conscious minds.
I try
to interpret them
with my head burrowed
beneath the quilts.
The snow is falling
on grandmother's house
coldness attracted by warmth
melting on the tin roof.
She talks
about grandfather—
his snow covered boots.
He is trapped
in the warmth
of her dream.
She moves her arms
up and down
against the covers
with a little-girl laugh.
Has she fallen back
into the snow?
Is she making angel wings?
Her movements become frantic.
"Grandmother," I cry out.
She is still.
And the snow clings
to the roof.
Her dreams freeze
to the pillow.

COMMUNION WITH THE DEAD

The dead didn't speak to me
when I was young
their voices silent
resembling sleep.
I'd get a glimpse of them
a shirttail in a memory
a hand at the edge of a dream.
Like unleavened bread
flat and thin
I washed them down
with a sip of cheap wine.

Now the dead speak
through radiator vents
streetlamps that buzz
the hum of a refrigerator.
They share stories about
my children and grandchildren,
discuss my latest surgery,
remedies for arthritis.
Like yeast bread
full and fragrant
they rise.
I toast them
with a glass of Bordeaux.

Sometimes they say, eat.

VISIONARY

The winter trees
look anorexic
in their brittle limbs,

silhouettes against
a graying sky,
the clouds a cataract

over the bright lens
of the sun.
I take a photograph

with my mind's eye,
winter colors muted
in black and white.

The late light shifts; I focus
on the sullen sheep, here—
the raucous crows, there.

I see it all as if
for the first time.
Earlier on this day

god spoke to me
in a white lab coat,
his voice as smooth

as the glass
on his slit-lamp microscope.
My mind railed

against his unholy word.
"You are blessed," he said.
"It is only in one eye."

Cyclops, I thought. Pirate.
The eye of God.
My pupils still dilated

as if high.
I see things differently now,
a seer in retrospect

with 20/20 hindsight.
I envision myself
as Milton or Homer,

but I know what I am—
a middle-aged woman
with no poem to call home.

EXPLOSION IN CAIRO

Who will inherit Mother's fine china,
crimson cardinals posed on delicate limbs?

Who will inherit Father's coin collection,
harmless metals smooth against the skin?

In the life they painted for me,
time was simply a slow measuring,

a leisurely ticking down
never expected to end—

certainly not by nameless men
whose language streams like curses.

Did my red hair tremble in a brighter hue
than my blood on the pavement?

C-WORDS

I hear *chemotherapy* and *corpse*
and *cadaver* when he gives me

the diagnosis. I imagine a single
entity, lonely at first, melancholy,

then angry, the anger exploding
into *chaotic* mitosis:

no longer
the little c-word, *cell*—

now the big c-word, *Cancer*.
I walk into Macy's,

buy a red scarf, wrap it
around my *cursing* mouth.

ON THE FIRST DAY OF HER 57TH YEAR

I woke in the morning and bees
stung my eyes. Happy Birthday:

this could be a bad one, I thought.
You can imagine the redness, stingers

floating near twin blue lakes.
Then, the girl inside, the one

who has inhabited this frail body
for more than half a century,

the one who cheers, *Never give up!*
even after cataracts and diabetes—

almost screamed. I tried to calm
her by recollecting old times, but my arm,

needled with sleep, demanded attention.
The girl in my nightgown stretched,

dragged her dirty robe to the bathroom
mirror, grabbed her mouthwash. When I stroked

her hair, bees gathered like an army,
hummed like marching soldiers.

And the girl who toasts me every birthday
with double-barreled bourbon whiskey

said: *Congratulations. We made it*
through another year.

THE HOUR AFTER MY DEATH

My body, a shadow under the elm tree,
sprawls unselfconsciously and without shame,

skirt hitched up over the left thigh,
cadaver-white limbs crushing the pliant grass.

A roll of belly fat protrudes over the waistband,
blouse billowing like a flag of surrender.

An ant wanders over a calloused heel.
One shoe missing—a pair of mismatched feet.

Oxygen surrounds me as if it matters,
but what choice does it have?

In my back yard, straight-legged crows
flock to angled limbs and wait.

How long before I am missed?
How long before a neighbor knocks

with gnarled fist on the screen door,
scatters the flies like water droplets,

calls a name I borrowed for a little while—
a name that means nothing to me now.

MISSING

The day your father disappeared
into the woods, we shelled peas
on the front porch. You wiped
your forehead on a yellow apron,
one blue pocket bulging, holding
what—? an extra hand?

That night, my father found him
straddling his shotgun like a lover.
A barn owl screeched. The moon
was a spotlight; the whites of his eyes
pleading.

INTENTIONS

The question arose
like crows fleeing a cornfield
air splitting into molecules
rising—a collective sigh.

Did he die by his own hand?

Whispers sift around this solemn occasion
trickle down beaded glasses of wine
shimmer and slide over lips.

We could not convince Mother to cremate you—
        to leave it at that.

Why the intrigue, Father?
You were always so easy to read.
With your furtive eyes,
you wore your guilt on your sleeve.

What we do know is this:
You entered the fields with a gun.
The crows were alive.
They flew in broken lines
startled by the sound of your passing
by the pull of a finger
intentional
        or not.

WAITING

We live in a house by the railroad tracks.
Grief coats the roof and windows,
grief covers the pine floors like dust.

A train whistles every two hours,
even at night, sullies our dreams.
When it rains, the yard swells.

Worms work their way to the surface
like words. My tongue probes at memories
like a chipped tooth.

I think of Father underground.
I think of empty spaces filling.
Can a man drown more than once?

The dust turns to mud, clings
to us like dead leaves. We scrub
our bodies raw. We are corpses

waiting to happen.

The House Laments the Loss of a Child

COVENANT

You swear you saw stars dancing on the ceiling;
that you smelled my perfume, sniffed again,
and it was gone. The crow on your dresser
screamed obscenities; you expected to die.

Night ends; your fever slithers away
like a snake out of Eden.
The sun licks the window panes.
You ring the bell—ask for water.

The flowers are wilted; dirt cracks beneath them.
I comb your hair, tangled like a bird's nest,
and count your breaths with each stroke.
You eat crackers; crumbs fall on the sheets.

Let the day slip by slowly now
as nimbus clouds cling to the sky.
Remember your promise at birth—
that I will leave this world first.

BULIMIC CREDO

I kneel before a porcelain font.
Sacrifice my daily bread.
Flush once, twice, with blue-
veined hand. The soul
is cleansed by water, blood.

Look at this temple, Mother.
How thin. How holy.

THINNING

1.

My daughter—
in a hospital gown
and alabaster skin—
steps on the scale,
her back to the numbers;
she doesn't look at me,
her head heavy
with the weight of her weightlessness.

Like the stick figures
she drew in kindergarten,
her filled out parts
have disappeared,
flesh stretched tautly
across her chest
like the fontanel
on a newborn's head,
heart fluttering visibly
in erratic beats.

This thinning began
with cervical effacement,
my womb's eagerness
to expel her into the glare
of inhospitable lights
(let the show begin—
the spotlight on her life);
the planes of her face
cast shadows,
the umbilical cord severed.

(She hungered
and my breasts were dry.)

2.

She steps off the scale,
her weight a frown
on the nurse's face.
For a moment
I forget that she is young
as she shuffles back to bed;
I kiss her goodbye—
her eyes accuse me
of what? of what? I ask.

I leave her
in this place of her beginnings.
I leave her and I am calm.

Tomorrow
the earth will move,
protest violently
against this unnatural
order of things;
the earth will move,
leave me with nothing
to hold onto.
8.3 on the Richter scale,
forever off balance.

I will look up
at the bruised sky
and the singed sun;
I will look up
and water the earth,
boundaries thinning
between earth and sky,
mothers and daughters,
sustenance and starvation.

(She hungered
and my breasts were dry.)

MISCARRIAGE

for Gina

Your tiny embryonic heart fluttered
like a hummingbird—and stopped.

You slipped away like liquid love.
Did you mistake my fear for reluctance?

From my window, the river winds
its jaundiced way around the cypress trees;

Spanish moss hangs like tangled
hair, the yellowed sun a bow.

Your bassinet chirps in the corner—
the song of a wounded bird.

DAUGHTER OF WATER AND AIR

I imagine it like this:
the lake
holding you down
with a heavy hand.
You sink
to sedimentary levels
then float, a bloated water lily
eutrophication ill-defined.
Air, not air.

Your soul
bursts into starlight
soaring past
this physical plane
of geometry, astronomy,
philosophy, theology
poking a hole
in the velvety fabric of night
pockets of light seeping through
thin, atmospheric layers.
Air, not air.

Shed your life
like skin that's grown too tight,
leaving it here, water bound
like an abandoned child,
but I am the abandoned one.
Boundaries blur, edges disappear—
after eons of motherhood
breathe, I say, breathe!
Air, not air.

RAIN

All day the rain
like a metaphor for grief
keeps me from looking up.

I fold into myself
under the silver droplets,
absorb the dampness.

Your yellow umbrella
with the pink polka dots
waits in the stand.

All day my palms
cup the rain
a cistern for my tears.

AFTER THE SUICIDE

"She seemed so happy," they say, gathered
around the casket. Hands flutter in front
of their faces, rumors whispered as fact.

They're grateful, for once, that their children
are there, though they're laughing inappropriately,
the girls flirting with the young men in dark suits,
somber ties.

"Shh," they mutter. "Show respect for the dead."
What they really mean is:
"Don't let her family hear you, see you,
acting *alive*."

They bow before the mother, her face slack
with grief, with drugs. The father stares
straight ahead, as if he can't bear to look
back. Can't bear to see what might have been.

THE HOUSE LAMENTS THE LOSS OF A CHILD

for Dr. Bruce Dennings

Who will listen
        to the house
at $150 an hour
        as it shifts its weight
on the plaid sofa
        shrugs its shutters
rearranges its shingles?

Who will hand it
        a tissue
stark white
        in a blue floral box?

AFTER IDENTIFYING HER CHILD AT THE MORGUE

She was alone for the first time
since her own umbilical cord was severed.
The steering wheel jerked in her gloved hands
and she struck a birch tree, white limbs
exposed under the glare of a baleful moon.

A patrolman painstakingly measures,
rubs his arms briskly, lights a cigarette,
shakes his head—breath crystallizing
in the frigid air. He thinks of distances,
thin threads, the way a life is measured.

That night he dreams: of how the snow
drank greedily with blood-stained lips;
of how the bitter moon gloated on the horizon—
a white blemish on the bruised sky—
so close, it blistered his thumb.

THE HUNT

My daughter takes off with the men
        stomping down her part of the woods
with laced up hiking boots
        and a gun in hand
trying to replace
        the son she cannot be.
He
        broke through the ice
on the pond last winter
        disappeared in his own black hole
swallowing cold
        spitting out his own warmth until emptied.
She was there
        helpless then, now guilt-ridden.
So she tracks off
        with her father
and an uncle
        to find the hole
marked just so
        on the side of a deer.
She'll come back
        tear-streaked or bloodstained.
I am not sure which.

BLACKBIRDS

She hangs shirts
        on the line
and sings
        for the lost child.
A feather drifts
        outside her womb.
It touches her
        flattened abdomen
which echoes
        like an empty drum.
She looks up
        and watches the blackbirds
fluttering like soot
        from ashes.
Back and forth
        in the wind
they wander.

Uncle

FOUR

Your zipper hums like a fly.
I pet the baby elephant's trunk.
The elephant sneezes; I flinch.
You wipe my hand on your sleeve.

DAISIES

I

am lying
on the cot.

His hand slides
up and down

up and down
against his skin.

The daisies
printed

on the panties
I wear

wilt.

DIRTY

Marie swipes cobwebs with a broom,
shakes the handle like a sword.
The sun spreads its yellow stain.

She strips the cot, bundles the dirty
sheets on the floor. My face feels flushed.
"What's wrong?" she asks. "What's wrong?"

Dust motes dance like fairies,
splay their legs.
Splay their legs.

BARE

This is what I remember:

your boots
scraping across the floor
bare naked floor
splinters rising to greet me
as I lie there
a weight
the weight of the world
on my chest
arms and legs
splayed
unlike a lover's.

My childhood
nailed to that floor
an offering
love come undone
a sacrifice
to your lust
uncle
a spark of madness
in your eyes
and death marching
quietly in mine.

ATTIC

What do I remember about the attic?
"The Twist." Dancing in bare feet.
A braided rainbow rug on a pine floor.
A lopsided window, the latch
rusted. The moon poised on a gray
pitched roof. Eyes that stared.

What do I remember?
The sound of his zipper—
how it hummed like a thousand
bees as they stung the soft flesh
between my thighs. How he
whispered, "Honey."

YOURS

This shyness is yours,
these averted eyes. Yours,

too, these dark dreams.
My veins, like rivers, flow

toward some unspoken ocean.
The hum in my throat

widens to a roar.
Is yours, too.

DEPRESSION

At times it's so heavy
we fear being crushed,

we think we will suffocate
unless the weight is lifted

and it starts to roll down
gentle hills that angle it

away from the gloomy apartment
and across the sagging bridge

onto the sturdy highway,
past the yield sign

and the white church downtown.
Below the hill, it slows to a stop

in front of the mental hospital.
Patients mill around outside.

For several weeks, I lived there.
From the fourth floor

I could see my uncle's cottage,
and on clear days, the red curtains.

Sometimes I could see him
landscaping the lawn,

loading a wheelbarrow.
How harmless he looked then,

moving heavy stones
from one side to another,

never permitting them to crush
the things he grew.

STONES

He pushes the gray wheelbarrow
filled with stones, and imagines

brains in a skull cavity.
Moving the pieces back and forth

in the yard, he considers where to do it.
Maybe in the fields behind the cottage

where the corn stands silent
and humble in the red dirt.

Then he remembers the crows—
their parched throats cawing; beady

eyes staring like Satan's sentinels.
And his father. How dirty he looked

on the ground.
Lifting another stone,

he places it by the rhododendrons,
their heads drooping in shame.

From dust to dust, he thinks.
Maybe his father had the right idea.

His eyes rest on the red curtains
beckoning in the chalky air.

He knows what's beyond that door—
the Oriental rug, plush and vibrant,

its swirls and floral patterns.
He imagines his blood seeping

into it, brain tissue scattering
like spilled stones.

PSYCHOLOGIST

From a fourth floor window, he can see
the uncle—can see the red curtains

flapping like birds' wings,
like a warning.

Bile rises in his throat and he washes
it down with bitter coffee.

Each night he dreams—
chases the uncle on uneven ground

through a labyrinth of corn
with harmless crows as witnesses.

He hears the click of the gun, feels
the recoil.

PERSPECTIVE

What you cannot see behind the red curtains
past the window sill
is the man shaking his head,
is the gun lying on the counter,
is the foot crushing the Oriental blossoms
scattered on a scuffed oak floor,
is the field mouse blinking in the corner,
is the memory of a record playing,
and a young boy's hips gyrating—
his father's laughter a crow cawing.

GRACE

Finally you will leave this life.
You recognize your name etched
in full upon the headstone,
the years falling away like grace.

Bask in the lingering light.
Make this your singular accomplishment:
Let your stone heart soften with remorse.
For one second. Just one.

BREATH

A gunshot startles the silence.
One breath lifts, then settles
like crows' wings.

UNCLE

with your penchant for my little girl panties,
with your tireless, roving fingers,
you pointed the gun *I* wanted to point,
pulled the trigger *I* wanted to pull.

Splattered blood and brain
on the Oriental rug,
painted Rorschach patterns
on the pristine wall.

Were you surprised
when your dark, impenitent eyes
encountered Satan's grin?

GRAVE

One stone,
a patch of rhododendrons,
a crow's oily wings
stained with death.
Even the gods must live
for days like this one.

HAINTS

Dear Ruth, have you heard about the haunted
attic in that old clapboard house—the one
I lived in with Daniel all those years—
nestled on the side of a mountain
like a hawk's nest? Jim, the handy man,
checked on the place like I asked.
Said he stood in the kitchen (with the sunny
yellow curtains and the rooster clock)
and heard music swirling from the attic.
Could have sworn it was "The Twist."
Said he climbed the rickety steps,
and opened the trap door. Said spider webs
shimmered in the sunlight like glitter.
Remember that oval rug you braided
for me in rainbow colors, maybe forty
summers ago now? It still covers
that unfinished pine wood floor—
the one with uneven planks and knots
that stared like eyes. The music stopped
as soon as Jim stepped on that floor.
He looked out the dormer window
at the garden—choked with weeds now—
window was latched shut. I bet the moon
still peeks in like a peeping Tom most nights.
And during the locust season, the droning
from the fields sounded like spaceships.
Jim said he turned around, felt goosebumps,
and saw a young man—a kind of outline
of a man—he swears it was a haint!
Thinks it was Ricky though he hated
bringing that up after the way he died and all.
When Daniel and I adopted that boy,
he was a mess. Dirty, half-starved. A shame
how that car wreck killed his mother,
and then his father—killing himself
in the cornfield. I still can't abide crows.
God only knows what else happened.

Ricky wasn't much of one to talk.
I think the past caught up with him.
I think that bullet was his ticket to peace.
He loved that attic. Read *The Hardy Boys*
and muscle magazines. Listened to 45s
and played with Daniel's granddaughter
up there—that shy little redhead with the curls.
A quiet one. I don't believe in haints,
do you, Ruth? Folks are haunted
by the past, not by half-visible souls
mucking around. Maybe Jim concocted
that story to give two old women a thrill!
Just us two now. Dusty and forgotten
in these decaying bodies—looking
like painted trolls when we have to see
the doctor. At night, we tend to fold ourselves
into bed like nightgowns in a dresser drawer,
granny gowns sewn from sensible
cotton and just a little lace on the fringes—
frayed, stained and yellow—the smell
of cedar under our bulbous noses.
Then something like this happens—
some crazy story or memory yanks
us out of that drawer, shakes us up a bit.
These days, I imagine Ricky in the afterlife
sitting on a porch swing drinking lemonade
and watching fireflies. Did you know
that the fireflies in heaven are the stars
we see at night? I bet the stars grow
weary of all the wishing that's done
on them. All I wish for nowadays is to die
in my sleep unaware, and in my prettiest
nightgown—the one with the yellow
daisies and green trim. Your sister, Marie.

HITCHHIKER*

My dead uncle is thumbing for a ride to Atlanta
as if his brain were still scheming from a solid gray skull,

(and not the skull splintered into pieces like a puzzle).
It's his hand movements that mark him as familiar

like a thousand other predators in disguise,
and I am shamed by those hands, thumb pointed skyward,

a memory so close, I tremble. My heart freezes
in response to him, as he blinks, then stares

only a short distance away. I am running from him
while stuck in time with him—a hellish reminder of the past.

My guilt remembers the attic cot; the shadow of him
in the dust-moted air—unable to escape from those hands.

In the dust-moted air—unable to escape from those hands,
my guilt remembers the attic cot; the shadow of him,

while stuck in time with him. A hellish reminder of the past
only a short distance away. I am running from him—

in response to him, as he blinks, then stares;
a memory so close, I tremble. My heart freezes,

and I am shamed by those hands. Thumb pointed skyward—
like a thousand other predators in disguise—

it's his hand movements that mark him as familiar
(and not the skull splintered into pieces like a puzzle).

As if his brain were still scheming from a solid gray skull,
my dead uncle is thumbing for a ride to Atlanta.

*Inspired by S. H. Lohmann's poem "Una Perdida: Santiago"

DREAMSCAPE

Some nights, even the moon
smothers its light. Feverish

stars blaze wildly. My uncle
and I trudge through the woods.

Wolves circle the piney grove,
eyes yellow against the dark.

An owl blinks, settles on a limb.
My uncle's hand is a paw clawing.

The owl's flight startles the air,
empties the grove of wisdom.

FLASHBACK

1. Each day the attic unfurls its tongue and I am lapped up inside.

2. Your head hovers above me, dust motes trembling in the air.

3. I live between therapy like a fragile bridge in a windy gorge.

4. I lie flattened, a dead end road paved by the past.

5. Each night the moon is an orifice filled with semen.

NIGHT

I see you
in the sleek black heads
of crows.
Those beady eyes
stare me into silence,
into a small
slip of a girl.
When the long night
trembles and nightmares
wet the sheets,
no one is safe.
Even the floorboards
ache with longing.

ASHES

Grandfather was hard of hearing,
cocked his head to one side like
the dog recognizing *treat* or *walk*.
A barking alarm, Peanut saved us
from fire.

It was the day after Christmas,
1960. The tree was brittle. I held
Grandfather's hand. The stars
tacked the night to the sky.

The house burned and burned.
We watched until sunrise
revealed blackened snow.
Grandfather wept, not for the house—
for Peanut, lost in the fire.

In the new house, Grandfather
never heard me crying; no dog
to sound the alarm. Prayers drifted
past the attic window, fell like ashes.

SECRET

What is hidden will be revealed.
—Gospel of Thomas, Saying 108

A spider's web catches
the dawn. A bird opens its beak
to the hesitant sun. I walk
the woods, memories chasing
me like hounds.
The past rises
like crows' wings—
the subtle beat
of a depraved man's heart.

SEPTEMBER

Every September I am the same
third-grader paralyzed in the night
by the same incessant dream—
my uncle trapping me in this new
house, this new state.

Relentless wind rattles the window panes;
autumn leaves curl up and die.
The moon closes its wide eyes.
Crows hunch their shoulders
and wait for morning's bruised arrival.

NINETY

Her eyes swim in blue
pools of grief whenever her
mind, floating like fog,
reaches out a tiny finger,
grasps a tendril of memory:
Ricky is dead—his life
snuffed out by his own hand.
Why are these people laughing,
singing? She knows the song.
She flinches from the sudden
shooting flames in front
of her, from the sweetness
wedged into her mouth.
Spit. That's the word. If
only she could *spit – it – out.*
A woman with graying red
hair kneels beside her.
Happy Birthday.
Marie closes her eyes,
sees a pine floor, a cot,
rumpled sheets, a record
going round and round,
circling like crows. Like
memories.

LIMBS

No matter where I go,
I am always in that attic.

No matter how many birthdays pass—
ten, twenty, fifty—

I am still four years old.
The gray pitched roof of memory

reminds me that I am alone,
that help *didn't* arrive—not then,

not now. In the dim light
behind my eyelids, I see

the child's panties, her legs
splayed and trembling

like leaves in a brisk wind,
limbs stripped bare like winter.

I should walk upstairs and cover her.
I should force the uncle to leave.

But I am not that woman.
I'm the woman who hides beneath

thread-bare sheets,
knees locked together.

SURVIVOR

In the white-out of a hospital room,
in the corner of an old sheet:
a blood stain.

Once I hallucinated in fear.
Now, heroically, my paper gown's
a cape.

In dreams I fly
with a visceral need
to forgive,

awaken to a crawl—
a hardened seed where I once grew
a heart.

Outside, innocent girls
in floral panties wait
to be rescued.

CROWS

For years, I saw him in my dreams.
For years, he interrupted my sleep,
a hunched crow scratching in the dirt.

The rain falls like stones, plunks
against the tin roof. The sky melts
like black wax. Listen.

There are dead men who still breathe—
dead men who smother the breath
of young hearts.

Imagine, I tell the therapist.
Imagine all we must let go of
just to hold on.

LINES

What I need to explain
is the feather I found.
And the crows that flew
over the telephone lines.
The single crow
I decided to curse as you.

How I finally learned your story,
the way your mother died on the highway,
the drunk driver in an eighteen-wheeler;
how your father's thoughts flapped
around like crows' wings, until what
had been a family unraveled
by chance, then design.

How I lay awake thinking
of you that night: at your
kitchen table with your steak
and beer, the Oriental rug beneath
your feet. Gun loaded, waiting.

My daughter is only three days old,
and I have thought of you all three.
It's still too early to know
if trust is a given thing,
if a curse can be released
like feathers in the wind.

God's Daughter Ushers in the End of the World

BIRTHING

took a lot out of the god
whose word was himself
separated darkness from light
land from sea
hung the sun and moon
poked stars in the sky
tossed down a fish
flung out a bird or two
cracked his knuckles
took a swig of beer
and really got down to work

fashioned bones and skin
fur and teeth
listened with a discerning ear
to squeaks and growls
barks and squeals
and in an exhaustive display
carved a pair
of naked feet
from dust
the mote
in god's eye

her body curved
a crescent moon
voluptuous woman
a star-gleam
in man's eye
the clock of time
ticked toward death
a downward spiral
while god rested
and rested
and perhaps rests still

ADVICE FOR EVE

Ignore the lush garden,
the fruit-laden tree,
a serpent that promises knowledge.

Strut past the ribald orangutan.
Swing your hips as if you own the place.
Stroll to the water's edge and gaze.

Tousle your hair; purse your lips.
Splay slender fingers over bare breasts,
areolas pointing toward heaven.

Sniff the primal scent of fecundity.
Examine that mysterious cleft.
Then, count your ribs, one by one.

Remember that number.

AND I BREATHE

The serpent came to me
iridescent scales reflecting a sun
newly birthed in a cerulean sky.
His eyes—green as the river Euphrates.

Unlike the other creatures of the garden
he spoke, his voice raw with power.
Words rippled over his tongue
like water over rocks,
seductive, empowering.

He appealed to my
reason, logic, intelligence.
His questions were *the* questions
stamped on my soul
almost from the moment
I was fashioned from that rib.

Why not eat of the tree?
I was bored—tired of being a helpmeet,
tired of being coddled by Adam,
tired of the soft-eyed animals
surrounding me.

Adam had already named the creatures
of this world.
He enjoyed our evening walks
with the Creator.
But I knew my place—
one step removed from
His breath
even in my beginnings.

What is Paradise
without the seeds of desire,
without the ability to create?
Was that my sin then,
the desire to create?

The tree stood alone in the midst
of the garden, its fruit heavy with
the weight of its knowledge.
Plucked, held loosely in my hand,
I took a bite.

What choice did I have?
To continue living as a demi-god—
one foot in heaven, the other in hell
for all of eternity?
To remain a slave to this garden
when I could be free
to the entire earth?

That bite plunged me
into an uncertain future,
one that winked at me, in the distance,
like the newly minted stars.

I handed the fruit to Adam.
He ate, fearful of being without me.
And that is when I understood:
I am the strong one.

Adam looks back at the cherubim—
their flaming swords cutting ribbons
into the night.
I step forward
into this new world,
one that remains to be named.

Outside the garden I see
the serpent slithering under a rock.
He looks back at me, winks,
and I breathe.

SATAN AND EVE

began as a human-shape
with bird wings
(before human and bird existed)
created to accompany God
to ooh and ahh
over His kindergarten
art—all those
millennia before He
mastered the world—
bird-winged beings rebelled
kicked out

listened (unlike God)
and held out
a well-shaped hand
thin fingers
tremble slightly
and innocent
luscious lips
bit down
eyes grew large
with knowledge—
evil

DEMONS

They assumed the position would be more sinful—
naked women and martinis. They'd participate
in cult sacrifices of children drenched in fear

and perform anti-miracles
that proved the power of Satan.
Humans would burn their churches

and synagogues, celebrate pagan rituals
without dressing them in disguises
like Christmas and Yom Kippur.

Shops would promote deviled eggs,
chocolate pitchforks, pointy tails
hot as jalapenos.

For awhile, they hung out with local
drug dealers, and once, helped shoot
an innocent by-stander (who survived).

But that required acrobatic moves—
took skill and patience.
"Why don't these thugs have target practice?"

one demon complained to another.
"Stray dogs, kittens, crows. Even the rank
garbage cans could fill in for a body."

They planned to lead young girls
into the hands of sex traffickers,
to erase any evidence left behind

by serial killers—like the one
who smoked unfiltered cigarettes
at the corner convenience store.

He'd be dead soon. Lung cancer.
They discussed the need for a replacement,
but then thought, *Why bother?*

Humans, it seemed, carried their own
inner demons. Even the pedophiles
could charm the wariest of mothers.

Instead, they crashed Halloween parties,
held dunked heads beneath the water for a few
seconds longer, apples bobbing by their ears.

At séances, they moaned in quivery falsettos,
blew out candles that whispered in the dark,
moved the pointer up and down on Ouija boards.

Finally, bored, they stopped looking for trouble,
shared cheap apartments and stale beer,
worked night shifts as bartenders, blackjack dealers.

Sometimes, on stormy afternoons,
you can hear them over the thunder
clinking beer mugs together

in the corner booth at the pizza parlor—
a picture of Boy, Tarzan and Jane
on the wall. Boy holds a thick

crust of pepperoni pizza on his lap
exactly where Tarzan's hand disappears.
They never tip the waitress.

Later, in black jeans and leather jackets,
they'll gather in front of the movie theater—
a murder of crows—umbrellas folded like clipped wings.

TIRED OF HUMAN

God grew up from fools and from under sinners,
like the ashes of incinerated angels
but they were always inside the clouds
the color of fire and of wounds
humming a song we forgot to learn.

I am tired of human
Howling in a stoup of holy water
'Love,' said God. 'Say, Love.'
There cannot be light without shadow.
He let himself believe it.

1. Raymond McDaniel, "Swamp Thing." *Saltwater Empire*
2. B.D. Love, "Strings From Nicaragua." *Water at the Women's Edge*
3. Jaki Shelton Green, "I know the grandmother one had hands." *Conjure Blues*
4. Ellen Bryant Voigt, "For My Father." *Messenger*
5. Terry L. Kennedy, "Tree of Smoke." *New River Breakdown*
6. Louise Glück, "Blue Rotunda." *Averno*
7. Natalie Kenvin, "The Old Queen Looks at Winter." *Bruise Theory*
8. Ted Hughes, "Crow's First Lesson," *Crow*
9. Barry Marks, "The Rabbi Visits Asia." *Sounding*
10. Elizabeth Arnold, "XX." *Effacement.*

EVE'S THOUGHTS IN THE AFTERLIFE

I hear the sermons, the rantings
in churches across the continents:
I was the weaker vessel.
I was easily deceived.
I should have trusted Adam.

They think I didn't trust?
I placed my hand
in the serpent's mouth and realized:
If truly I belong to Man,
why was there no ring on my finger?

GOD'S DAUGHTER USHERS IN THE END OF THE WORLD

I am no deity, although Eve was fashioned
in my image. I sweep the stars free of debris.

My cloud slippers slide on heaven's floor.
When I peer through kaleidoscopic layers,

galaxies reflect in my eyes. Father motions me
to His side. He's bored. Again. Time for Scrabble.

We play games that don't require the spoken
word (for His Word leads to creation).

Brother used to play. Now, he mumbles,
counts fishes and loaves over and over

like a confused restaurateur. He was fun
before the Man gig. I think he's still sore

over that little fiasco. Tonight, our Father
appears to be tired and preoccupied, moving

iridescent letters across a moonlit board.
When He's worried, to whom can He pray?

Sweat stains His glistening white robes,
blood drips onto the star-studded floor.

When He stitched the stars to the Milky Way,
His fingers bled for an entire millennium.

Lately, He has been working overtime,
frantically stitching icebergs to the ocean

floor. Brother swears He is wasting
His time. Later tonight, Father will enact

a new plan—create apocalyptic dreams to
disturb the sleep of poets. Brother approves.

“Change begins with co-creators,” he says,
rubbing the holes in his palms absently.

I concentrate on the game. When I win
(which isn’t often), Father creates

in accordance with my words. Last time,
it was *dolphins* and *butterflies*.

Adam and Eve (what innocents they were!)
celebrated for days. The game is almost over.

Father spells *CHRIST*. Brother winces.
I play the last word: *A...N...T...I.*

Plight

TRAVELOGUES OF A DYSFUNCTIONAL FAMILY*

I. Plane: Daughter

Nothing quite like popping a Xanax on a red-eye
after losing your virginity.

*

The attendant has a James Bond look, his tie clip
a set of wings. Probably a hidden camera.

*

My boyfriend wanted the lights on—"To see you,"
he said. I was feeling insecure.

*

Maybe I'll imitate Bond or that brazen redhead at
the ticket counter—her hair a poppy field.

*

My therapist hung a sign over his desk: *Act as if.*
Careful, Dr. D.—transference is likely.

II. Cab: Mother

Nothing quite like hailing a cab in a monsoon
with 45-year-old legs.

*

Never mind; the cabbie's an old geezer, angling
the mirror to check out my breasts.

*

My lover has been pouting for a threesome:
"Imagine all of the delicious arms and legs!"

*

I'm thinking of flashing the cabbie or maybe
the stud at the corner, his umbrella a Freudian cigar.

*

My hairdresser thinks he's a poet: "Let's cover the gray and play."
Get to it, Jacques, before my mother stares back in the mirror.

III. Bus: Son

Nothing quite like a cottonmouth hangover
on a bus hurtling through the desert.

*

The driver aims for the pot holes like a
video game champ. I swear he's a sadist.

*

My girlfriend wants to "cool it" with the sex.
What? She's married to Jesus now?

*

Maybe I'll punch out the driver or the marine
across the aisle, with that landing strip crewcut.

*

My mother leaves post-it notes on the refrigerator:
"Take out the trash." Watch out. The garbage men cometh.

IV. Train: Father

Nothing quite like getting a black eye
on a train after fighting a mime.

*

At least the balding porter has a good
sense of humor: "Did he scream?"

*

My ex enjoys playing the martyr. Then again,
I think I'm God.

*

Wonder if I should befriend the porter or the
scholarly brunette, her laptop a security blanket.

*

My boss wants nonviolent solutions. "When in doubt,
talk it out." But mimes don't talk, testosterone does.

*Inspired by Heather Hartley's poem, "Bulkhead Chronicle"

BIPOLAR

You told me two things when we talked on the phone:
If you could be anyone, you'd be Van Gogh, and
The walls in your ward are the color of weak tea.

It was the first week of your hospitalization.
When I visited, you stared at the ceiling,
Tapped your socks on the floor, your arms
Puckered with scars.

Later, we played cards with a stained deck,
Kept the Jokers. You counted backwards
From a thousand to prove you were well.
It stormed that night—thunder scolded the mountains.

In your apartment, the kitchen trash held a fistful of hair.
I was afraid to look at your paintings, canvasses facing the wall.
In my dreams, they tumbled like dominoes.

PLIGHT

Needles pierce hands, feet and brow; back arches against the wood.
Mary hands you her breast; you suckle like a pig.

Soar over earth's swollen belly; follow the flight patterns of birds.
Swallow the psychotropic pill; land on fragile, taloned feet.

Normal wears comfortable shoes, sits on a wall, solid as gray stone.
Doesn't redesign skin, take the silver blade, pare self to glistening bone.

A BIPOLAR CRISIS

Demands immediate attention, like a fragile
Egg perched on the edge of the counter, in danger of
Falling onto the white tiled floor,
Gracelessly plummeting. Your scattered thoughts are
Hell. Your urge to cut, to feel the sting, to bleed,
Ironically, isn't a death wish, but proof that you're real.
Just lie still. Relax, says the EMT,
Kindness showing in his eyes. You wonder if he
Loves a daughter, close to your age, or
Maybe a son, one who plays football, one who
Never gives him a reason to worry.
Outside, neighbors watch the ambulance
Pull out of the parking lot. Sirens pierce the once
Quiet night. The ambulance bounces over the
Rough road. The EMT applies pressure to the wound.
Stupid, your mind screams. You hadn't meant
To cut so deeply, but this time—bone.
Unable to keep looking in the man's eyes, unwilling to be
Visible, you close your own. Another stint in the psych
Ward, you think. Who'll be there this time? Jesus? Superman with his
X-ray vision? And you hate the walls—that maddening green. Never
Yellow—the color of egg yolks, daffodils, or your mother's favorite,
Zinnias. You recall your pulse jumping, your blood a river, the blade a silver fish.

VISITING HOUR

My daughter will say she has no memory
of the courtyard, the budding dogwoods,

the cardinal watching from a thin branch,
heart fluttering in his tiny chest.

She doesn't remember her hand against the window,
the window tinted, not meant for seeing or being seen.

One month that spring, I drove two hours each
way, and waited in the courtyard. An elderly couple

sat on a wrought iron bench—the man picked
blossoms with a weathered hand.

Every night I stood before that locked
door at six o'clock, the visiting hour.

I followed others, shared the same reluctant
shuffle down green corridors to "Betty's Place"—

the cafeteria where my daughter ate salads
and sandwiches, and avoided the guards' eyes.

Hunched over the Formica table, we sat
in aluminum chairs the color of putty,

her eyes glazed with the drug of indifference,
hair dirty, clothes hanging on her small frame.

Sometimes, a low keening interrupted our visits—
a pummeling of fists, a new patient in an antiseptic gown.

I took magazines, *Discover* and *The Artist*,
American Photo and *The Scientific American*.

Bizarre cover photos of brains, the Milky Way,
black and white horses in a rainbow lake.

Sitting in the courtyard, I removed the staples,
offered her loose pages she could shift,

could rearrange to form new stories.
She has no recollection of these gifts.

Bits and pieces of the past were shocked
out of her along with the depression.

I imagine giving her the gift of memory—
of the lone cardinal preening, his wings

spreading crimson against the white
blossoms—her mouth a surprised O.

HALLUCINATION

Tonight, even the birds
walk overhead. The moon

bursts into a billion stars,
and the curve of the sky

threatens my sanity. Clouds
beckon me to a field

full of crows, their beaks
hold the eyes of the gods—

some open, some closed.

FOR YOU WHO CHOSE SUICIDE

For you, mere survival was inadequate;
you needed to silence your demons.

In time, wisdom would have shared
its definition of self—
of learning how to live among them.

How many times did you ravage
your flesh as if to exorcise
that rage, cut below layers
of skin, carve rivers born
of blood, of circumstance?

What good is rage
when it leads to this—
a closed casket at the front of a church,
the Christ child staring blankly,
a broken mother?

She must bury you now,
shield you from the polemical crows,
staunch the bleeding one last time.

IN THE PSYCH WARD

When the walls melt, form sticky
piles on the floor, and paper gowns
sag like skin, no one is young.
Looking in a mirror destroys
another illusion.

But there *are* no mirrors—
only blank eyes that reflect
whatever drugs they hand out—
slick capsules in paper cups.
Everything's paper here.

NOTICE

When my daughter disappeared,
volunteers didn't gather to search the mountains,

never scoured hiking trails, woods dotted with lilacs.
Her name wasn't mentioned on the local news

or the front page of the paper. Her face
never graced milk cartons, full-paged

ads, billboards. Dogs didn't sniff the grass,
her dirty clothing, never hunted her scent.

Police weren't called; no one questioned.
No notice posted on the Internet or bulletin

boards. She was never labeled *missing*.
When my daughter disappeared,

mutated into a quiet creature with scarred
wrists, bald spots parting her brown hair,

no one spoke of her.
Even the crows didn't notice.

ON VISITING MY BROTHER IN A MENTAL INSTITUTION

If I could love you
        out of your madness
coax you into the light
        a vampire no longer cursed
you could come home.

But the madness defines you
        leaves you without boundaries
like a homeless man
        you have no place to go
but anywhere.

You tell me
        that a man without a country
can not lose his way
        your thoughts can be
as elusive as light on water.

I smile
        as you light a cigarette
your smoke softening the edges
        of these hard rock walls
this prison for homeless souls.

Come home, brother.
        Soon.

1969: THE YEAR OF MOTHER'S GREAT DEPRESSION

That year, instead of children,
weeds grew in our house—
painted the floors with dirt,
spewed oxygen into breathless lungs,
crushed our flowering desires,
stalked past the ash-colored roof
and cursed an indifferent sun.

HOW TO COPE WITH A CRAZY MOTHER

Answer the phone.
Vow never to answer the phone again.
Search for signs of your own madness
the way you search for wrinkles under fluorescent lights.
Turn off the lights.
Worry about your daughters—your gifts to them.
Renew that prescription.
Make an appointment with your therapist.
"She is a crazy-maker," you sigh, like
the privileged middle-class woman you are.
Pop a pill.
Open your mouth wide, wider.
"You're still grinding your teeth," notes your dentist.
Bite the hand that feeds you.
Apologize.
Apologize, again.
"Sometimes, I hate her," you confess to your best friend,
tears salting the margaritas.
Read *Psychology Today* — nature versus nurture and epigenetics.
Pop another pill.
Dream of her as a child.
See the alcoholic father, the weak mother.
Feel the fleshy, sweaty palms.
Hear the hitched breathing.
Smell the chlorinated pool. (What pool?)
Taste the truth like bitter almonds.
Wake up.
Forgive for the seventieth times seventh time.
Answer the phone.

MOTHER'S MORNING PHILOSOPHY

The slow motion of her heart
left us bereft of love.

Bowls and cups on the Formica table
awaited us each morning.

Cigarette smoke plumed the air. She served
spoonfuls of nihilism for breakfast.

THE LAST MORNING

At breakfast in the messy dark gloom of the kitchen,
I stare at my mother who smokes while I eat.

I tremble a smile, then ask for the juice;
over the thunder, I can't hear her speak.

Just love me, please love me, my eyes beg,
as her smoke trails loosely in the air.

"You'll never no never know how I feel.
It's a knife in my gut, this blood we don't share."

The clock counts down to the thunder
like a dream that gets crushed from behind:

she purses her lips, snuffs out her cigarette,
and passes the juice one last time.

PATTERNS

I saw mother
        in the dream
standing out
        against blurred walls
cutting across
        my room.
Mother
        in her yellow negligee
a singing canary
        yellow with age.
She came with
        silver scissors
to cut me
        into her shape.
Strength in her feathered hands
        eyes fluttering
the scissors cut
        across my back
sharp
        slitting the seams.
I wake
        and she flees
my room.

WHO(LE)

my mother my mother my mother she
who'd lost God in the same fire as the tooth fairy,
Offer me your prayers, those white
scars, scars. And not just mothers.
We have heard the poets long dead
the unlucky dead and the lucky dreaming,
she was not I, she was not my mother,
because I am shattered.
Do you know what I look like?
I made myself a circle, then a square.

1. Ellen Bryant Voigt, "My Mother." *Headwaters*
2. Megan Falley, "The First (Noel)." *After the Witch Hunt*
3. Sandra Beasley, "Heretic." *Theories of Falling*
4. Ingrid de Kok, "Letter from Childhood." *Seasonal Fires*
5. Billy Collins, "Lines Composed Over Three Thousand Miles from Tintern Abbey." *Picnic, Lightning*
6. Jim Murphy, "Stranger, Field and Horse." *The Uniform House*
7. Sharon Olds, "Still Life in Landscape." *The Unswept Room*
8. Louise Glück, "The Red Poppy." *The Wild Iris*
9. Angela Ball, "That Was Me." *Night Clerk at the Hotel of Both Worlds*
10. Lisa Williams, "Geometry." *Woman Reading to the Sea.*

Casting the Bones

THE BLUE GOOSE CAFÉ

I am loving you
        in the Blue Goose Café
right here in the dead heart
        of Texas
right here where a beloved President
        was slaughtered
in the midst of black gold
        in this city of fallen gods
where all is dark beneath the surface
        and glass houses beg: *no more stones.*

The ceiling fans stir yesterday's newspapers.
        The greasy bartender yells—*Old news is good news,*
and I laugh at the clichés:
        the wobbly ceiling fans and bar stools,
the little tables neatly arranged outside
        in the unseasonably warm February sunshine.
And then at you,
        toasting me with a red plastic cup,
wooing me with your sunbaked face,
        your smoldering smile.

FIRST KISS

He was older—a real man.
I was sixteen with coltish
legs and eyes that followed
the stubble on his chin. The dark
shadows were a mystery to me—
not my father's reassuring whiskers,
but something dangerous.

He drove a tan truck, carried a gun
and a camera—a detective for hire who shot
photographs of cheating husbands and wives.
In suburban neighborhoods, I sat with him,
a congenial spy. Lamplight spilled
through innocent windows. He cursed
when the blinds closed.

He leaned forward. The wait was over.
Cicadas chirped. Tree frogs croaked
their mating calls. Leaves skittered
across the sidewalk. The scent of coffee
and spearmint gum closed the distance
between us. Night folded me in her arms.
The streetlight flickered like an eyelid.

CASTING THE BONES

She dreams, enters the spirit world,
hovers near the window, searches
the night sky for Octans and Orion.
The moon beckons, a curved finger.

Reader of tea leaves, observer of bed
sheets spread like tarot cards across a table.
Seeker of owls, oracles, omens,
palms supplicant, a gypsy wanderer.

Her eyes follow her lover's bones,
an indentation on the left side of the mattress.
Like a chalk outline at a murder scene—
legs splayed, an archer's bow.

Her eyes shift to the right side
where she observes her own bones
tilting the night like the crescent moon
or an embryo curled within a womb.

Like an African soothsayer, she interprets
the bones cast before her,
measures the distance between them,
invisible seams that divide.

UNHINGED

Words tumbled in the air like leaves
the year we lived in autumn,

our voices rusty like the hinge
on the pantry door. I'd pry it open,

search for popcorn, anything that made
noise—or at least a burst of effort.

We'd sit on the brown leather sofa,
your amber drink an elixir,

my popcorn a wall of sound. We'd sigh;
inconsolably mourn the differences

that had attracted us those early years—
green-leafed with expectation.

Sometimes, we'd jabber nervously
like alarmed crows, aware that words,

sharp as talons, could serrate
the denial between us.

I lost flesh that year, although my face,
bloated from popcorn and tears,

stared back at me, an unhinged
moon in the bathroom mirror.

INCLEMENT WEATHER

The sky ripens like a plum
        clouds bloated and pregnant with rain
lightning streaks across the sky
        without resistance.
Reminds me of what we've become
        settled in our separate lives—
like old folks in nursing homes
        time dictates our stale routines;
I read a book: You watch TV,
        our faces bathed in bluish light.
Thunder rolls across these hills,
        echoes of a passionate time
when we made heat, electrically charged
        opposite poles meeting in delight.
Now we shuffle off to bed
        our backs construct invisible walls
I hear you breathing
        your rhythmic snores;
the house shudders against the night
        thunder opens up the sky
I feel the wetness on my cheek
        and wonder that it ever rains
upon this dry, arid place.
        A hollow longing in the night
covers us like thinning sheets
        and leaves me shivering.

IT IS THE DEATH OF SUMMER

It is the death of summer, when red-
veined leaves waft past chimneys,
skitter nervously to the ground.
And whether you toast marshmallows
in the fire or heat the kettle for tea

you are not here.

Do you know
it is the death of summer, that the red-
veined wings of cardinals
flit from limb to limb,
settle patiently and wait?

THE HUM OF THE EARTH

Scientists say
  the earth hums
emits a buzzing
  like a mosquito
    in a jar—
droning that's below
  the range of human hearing.

They say
  ocean waves
produce the hum
  by crashing over continental shelves.
They collide and send
  a cacophony
    to the seafloor.
Vibrations ripple—
  the earth hums.

They say
  hurricanes and tsunamis
generate their own hum,
  which is why animals
seek shelter
  before their worlds fall apart.
Perhaps they hear
  the hum of the earth.

I, too, have heard
  the hum of the earth,
its low song beckoning me
  in that moment before sleep—
you know the one—
  you hear your name called
urgently, then silence.

I heard it, too,
        in the air
before the words you spoke
        at the moment of your leaving.
And like the animals, I huddled
        in a dark corner
yearning for higher ground
        crouching, listening, listening.

RUSH HOUR OVER THE MARSH

Brimming with life since prehistoric times,
the marsh exhales a sweet bouquet.

A cloying scent of death and life,
where pelicans bow to the cyclic moon.

We commute en masse to modern caves,
burn fossil fuels in acrid air.

Primitive beasts that prey upon the night,
we scurry to and fro across the bridge.

SLEEP ON A CLOTHESLINE

Night paints the sky with a star-spattered brush.
It's me it's painting for.
Palm trees linger in the light of the moon.
Sand crabs tickle my feet.
A mullet splashes like it hasn't a care.
The stench of dead fish wafts under my nose
and settles on my tongue like week-old gumbo.
Night smells the way a train sounded
whistling in my ears:
a whistle blown by Katie Kelleher
in Ocean Springs, Mississippi, at Fort Maurepas
because we were boisterous in 2005.
We *thought* we were boisterous in 2005.
Hurricanes battered old mansions and oaks,
and lanterns chased shadows from the windows
though none of us could see.
None of us had x-ray vision
because we were short and short-sighted.
Sleep on a clothesline, the meteorologist advised.
The silver scissors of madness and fate
cut up all of our dreams.
We were about as lighthearted as landmines.
We hid under tree trunks
and spit up oceans in our sleep.
Little Faith was afraid of swimming alone,
so tonight, tomorrow, and with every full moon,
she will ride a rabid dolphin in the Gulf of Mexico.
She will venture so far out, so far away from the shore,
I'll have to start looking for her before she is born.
Sic transit gloria mundi.
Watch as the stars stick out their tongues.
Watch as the seagulls slip off their socks.
Watch as the glorious star-spattered night
spills over us, covers us, all.

AFTER KATRINA

We live in a house crippled by desire.
The bottom half is missing, a magician's trick—
a sleight of nature's hand.
Mud covers the foundation
but not our fear. On the second floor,
three bedrooms and a bathroom pose
as home. Outside, my wedding dress
hangs from an oak, a ghoulish lynching.

On nostalgic days, we dig in the yard,
seekers of lost treasure—tarnished
spoons, faceless photographs—
we recognize our children by their clothing,
their want. When rain pounds the blue-tarped
roof and the bayou rises, we close
the curtains, circle the lanterns,
pray the wind's a benevolent ghost.

HOW WE BURY OUR DEAD

Mattresses slump over the cemetery fence
begging for entry to our burial grounds.
Defeated by flood waters and mud
they sag against the sweltering heat.

Mother's funeral drones on and on
as the minister's voice mingles with
flies and mosquitoes, their hums
mating with misery.

Mother stayed
with her potbellied pig—
Rosie couldn't evacuate—
stayed in her house of sticks.
Hadn't she heard of the big bad wolf?
Katrina howled and was hungry.

What fear she must have felt
as the roof collapsed,
what fear as she clung
to Rosie's quivering neck.
The wolf howled for hours,
not a brick house in sight.

The minister's words drip
in liquid air.
We blink. We breathe.
Open and close. In and out.
Open and close. In and out.
Heads bowed with the weight
of what is gone.

Hawaiian flowers bloom
across our chests, flip flops
brash against the mire
pink and green, pink and green
Angels avert their eyes at such brightness.
We wear donations from the kindhearted.

We leave
through an unhinged gate
climb into our borrowed cars
pick our way through the wolf's lair
stick houses piled like funeral pyres.
Ghosts sift through their mangled pasts
while hope sits quietly on the curb.

This is how we bury our dead
on a Mississippi day in September.

Acknowledgments

Special thanks to everyone who helped bring this book to fruition. I am especially grateful to my talented writing group for their suggestions and encouragement: Bev Blasingame, Cynthia Tanner, Valerie Winn, Mary Ann Avallone-O'Gorman, Emily Rhinelander, Jennifer Moffett, Judy Dalgo, James Murphy, Douglas Myatt, Michelle Ladner, and Elaine Stevens.

Many thanks, also, to my friend, Gina Morgan, for her down-to-earth suggestions and unfaltering support.

I am also indebted to my mentor, friend, and former creative writing professor, Dr. Claude (Bud) Clayton Smith, who believed in me in my youth, and then again, some 35 years later. His practical and inspirational comments were invaluable.

Love and appreciation for my supportive husband, Frank, who willingly became "a book widower" for the duration of this project.

Much love and gratitude for my daughters to whom this book is dedicated: Megan inspired me by sharing the work of talented poets. Katie encouraged me to identify myself as a writer, *first*—the best writing advice I've ever received.

Also, thanks to my family of origin—parents, siblings, grandparents, aunts, uncles, cousins—for love, laughter, memories, and yes, for a crazy and colorful past.

And finally, thanks to my publisher, Dr. Sue Brannan Walker, who instilled me with confidence from the moment she read that first poem. Simply put, this book wouldn't exist without her.

Grateful acknowledgment is made to the following publications in which the listed poems (some in slightly different form) have appeared: *Negative Capability, Volume 34: The Body in D[ist]ress*: "A Bipolar Crisis"; *The Awakenings Review*: "Bare" (previously titled "Childhood"); "Blackbirds"; "The House Laments the Loss of a Child"; "How We Bury Our Dead" and "On Visiting My Brother in a Mental Institution"; *Katrina Memories*: "After Katrina" and "How We Bury Our Dead"; *The Alalitcom*: "Covenant"; *The*

Magnolia Quarterly and *The Mississippi Press*: "Interpreter of Dreams"; *Independent Review*: "The Hunt."

The following poems (some in slightly different form) placed in writing competitions: The Alabama Writers' Conclave competition: "Covenant" (3rd place); William Faulkner-William Wisdom competition: "Sleep on a Clothesline" (Finalist); "Bare" (previously titled "Childhood," Short List); "How We Bury Our Dead" (Semi-Finalist); *The Magnolia Quarterly* competition: "Interpreter of Dreams" (2nd place), *Independent Review* competition: "The Hunt" (3rd place).

About the Author

FAITH GARBIN

Author photo by Lyndsey Richardson - Richardson Studios

Faith Garbin lives on the Gulf Coast in Ocean Springs, Mississippi, with her husband, Frank. Although poetry is her first love, she also writes creative nonfiction and short stories. Her work has appeared in *Negative Capability, Volume 34: The Body in D[ist]ress, Katrina Memories, The Awakenings Review,* and *Imagine This! An ArtPrize Anthology,* among others. A co-founder of Women of Words (WOW), she is also a member of the Poetry Society of America, the Mississippi Poetry Society, the Gulf Coast Writers' Association, and the Alabama Writers' Conclave. She has been a finalist in the Pirate's Alley Faulkner Society's Creative Writing Competition in the poetry and essay categories. Her degree is in English from Virginia Tech. She has two daughters and twin granddaughters. Her website is www.faithgarbin.com.

KATIE KELLEHER – COVER PHOTOGRAPHER

Katie Kelleher is a freelance artist and photographer living in Asheville, North Carolina. She spends much of her time searching dumpsters, scrap piles and alleyways for scenes or materials with the potential to become something beautiful. She tends to casually overlook this mention when first meeting people. Her work has been featured in publications and galleries internationally. When not creating art, she can usually be found hiking with her dog Journey, rock climbing in the beautiful surrounding mountains, playing soccer, or wondering why she sounds so much more interesting on paper. Her website is www.followtheartstrings.weebly.com

Made in the USA
Charleston, SC
02 August 2016